11+ Super Selective Maths: 30 Advanced Questions

Book 1

The 11+ Company

Published by The 11+ Company
34 Priory Road
Richmond
TW9 3DF
UNITED KINGDOM

Telephone: +44 (0)20 3667 3600
Email: enquiries@the11pluscompany.co.uk
Website: www.the11pluscompany.co.uk

First published in Great Britain in 2014
Copyright © The 11+ Company 2014

ISBN: 978-0-9928958-0-8

British Library Cataloguing in Publication Data
A CIP catalogue record for this book is available from the British Library.

Acknowledgements:

Text by Cavelle Creightney, PhD

Cover Design, Page Layout & Editing by Spiffing Covers

Subject Specialist Editing by Richard E. Martin, PhD Eng.

About This Book

The **11+ Super Selective MATHS** series has been written especially for children who seek 'more than ordinary' mathematical challenges. Filled with questions designed to stimulate thinking rather than simply elicit learned responses, this series provides the challenge that able pupils seek. Selective UK secondary schools are increasingly developing entrance exams that test potential rather than coached learning. As such we do not offer any particular exam format (e.g. CEM Durham, GL Assessment). Instead children's learning will be brought to life by our questions that demand insight and grasp of the fundamental concepts underlying each problem. Our fully worked answers demonstrate different strategies for solving 11+ mathematical challenges. Attractively designed and with ample space inside for pupils to express their working, this series will lead pupils to discover the fun, beauty and elegance of Mathematics!

There are three books in the **11+ Super Selective MATHS** series. Each book
- Contains 30 stimulating numerical and mathematical reasoning challenges
- Provides advanced practice material in mathematical thinking at 11+
- Includes fully worked answers & explanations
- Is suitable for use at the very top end of Key Stage 2 and at Key Stage 3
- Is suitable for practice for scholarship exams and at 13+

About Our Authors
All our authors are highly qualified graduates and subject specialists from leading UK universities.

Question 1

Jason arranges five white cubes into the sculpture shown below from two different view-points.

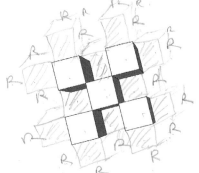 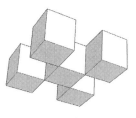

He then decides to glue black cubes, which are the same size as his white cubes, to **all the exposed faces** of his sculpture.

(a) How many black cubes will he need?

*Answer:*_____

Jason later decides to expand his black sculpture by gluing red cubes, which are the same size as his white and black cubes, to **all the exposed faces** of his black sculpture.

(b) How many red cubes will he need?

*Answer:*_____

Question 2

whole number   *next to*

In an 8-digit numerical code all the digits are **positive integers**. Each group of six adjacent digits adds to 24 and each group of five adjacent digits adds to 20.

(a) What is the sum of all eight digits?

Answer:_____

(b) How many possible combinations of positive integers can the 4th and 5th digits represent?

Answer:_____

Maria arranges the following five pairs of letters - *a, a; b, b; c, c; d, d;* and *e, e* - according to the following rules. The two *a*'s are next to each other, the two *b*'s are separated by one letter, the two *c*'s are separated by two letters, the two *d*'s are separated by 3 letters and the two *e*'s are separated by 4 letters. The list starts with a *d* followed by an *e*.

(c) Can you write down the complete list in the correct order?

Answer:_____

Question 3

(a) A lighthouse flashes every four seconds, a second lighthouse flashes every five seconds, a third lighthouse flashes every six seconds and a fourth lighthouse flashes every seven seconds. If they all start flashing at exactly the same time at midnight, at what time will they all flash together again?

*Answer:*_____

(b) Maria plays football in the park every day, Jonah plays every second day, Anna plays every third day, Christopher plays every fourth day, Karim plays every fifth day and Luke plays every sixth day. The last time they all played together was on Maria's birthday, the 21st of March. On what date will they all play together again?

*Answer:*_____

Question 4

Each of the symbols below has a value associated with it. No symbol has more than one value and no two symbols have the same value. You can add the values of all the symbols in any given row or column. This gives you the total value for that row or column.

	♥	◉	◉	100
◉		◉	♥	100
◉	✓	✓	♥	X
♥	✓	✓		124
100	124	132	Y	

Work out the value of each symbol and then find the values of **X** and **Y**.

◉ = _____   ♥ = _____   ✓ = _____   **X** = _____   **Y** = _____

Question 5

Two planes fly along the same flight path in opposite directions.

- Plane A flies from Island A to Island B while plane B flies from Island B to Island A.
- Plane B flies at an average speed of 240 km/hour.
- Both planes pass each other after plane A has been flying for 30 minutes.
- 10 minutes later plane B still has 20 km left to reach Island A while plane A lands at Island B.

(a) What is the distance between the two islands?

*Answer:*_____

(b) If plane A departed from Island A at 14:20, at what time did plane B depart from Island B?

*Answer:*_____

Question 6

A manufacturer of widgets must order the correct number of crates for packing the widgets in before they can be shipped to their final destination.

Each crate holds exactly 570 widgets.

11,097,303 crates were initially ordered for 6,325,463,254 widgets.

A further 9,144,078 crates were later ordered for an extra 5,212,124,876 widgets.

You are given the following information.

Widgets		Widgets		Crates		Widgets
6,325,463,254	÷	570	=	11,097,303	remainder	544
5,212,124,876	÷	570	=	9,144,078	remainder	416
11,537,588,130	÷	570	=	20,241,381	remainder	960
			=	20,241,382	remainder	390
2,835,678,321	÷	570	=	4,974,874	remainder	141

Use the information given above to help you answer the following questions. **Do not perform the divisions or use a calculator.**

(a) How many widgets are still without crates?

*Answer:*_____

(b) How many more crates are required for all the widgets to be packed?

*Answer:*_____

(c) What is the total number of crates required for all the widgets?

*Answer:*_____

It is later discovered that 2,835,678,321 widgets are damaged and will no longer be shipped.

(d) What's the total number of crates now required?

*Answer:*_____

(e) How many widgets does the last crate contain?

*Answer:*_____

The production manager discovers that she has made an error in her calculations and in fact the number of damaged widgets is 2,835,678,721.

(f) How many crates in total will be required in the final analysis?

*Answer:*_____

(g) How many widgets does the last crate now contain?

*Answer:*_____

Question 7

The radii, r, of a set of concentric circles are in the ratios of 1:2:3:4:5:6 and the radius of the smallest circle is 9 cm (*see picture below - not drawn to scale*). You are told that the area of a circle is πr^2 and π = 'pi' = 22/7.

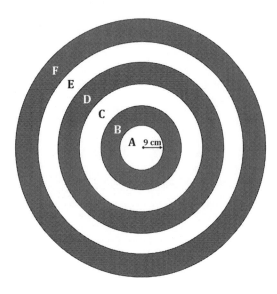

(a) What is the radius of circle D?

*Answer:*_____

(b) Calculate the area of the largest shaded part?

*Answer:*_____

(c) You are told that the perimeter of a circle is $2\pi r$, where r is the radius of the circle and π = 'pi' = 22/7. Calculate the total perimeter of all the circles.

*Answer:*_____

Question 8

In the table below, each symbol is associated with one (and no more than one) digit between 0 and 9, and no two symbols share the same digit.

▮ × ▮ = ⊞	⊙ × ✚ = ▮ ▲	⊙ × ◇ = ⊙
⊕ × ⊕ = ▮ ⊕	▲ × ▲ = ✚	Φ × ♥ = ♥
⊕ × ▮ = ◇ ⊙	✚ × ✚ = ◇ ⊕	Φ × Φ = ✚ ⊞
⊙ × ▮ = ▲ ✚	✚ × ✚ × ✚ = ⊕ ✚	Δ × ◇ = Δ
✚ × ▲ = ⊙	▲ × ⊙ × ✚ = ⊕ ✚	Δ × ▲ = ◇ ♥

Use the relationships shown above to work out the digit that corresponds to each symbol.

▲	=	_____	◇	=	_____
⊙	=	_____	⊞	=	_____
♥	=	_____	Φ	=	_____
▮	=	_____	✚	=	_____
⊕	=	_____	Δ	=	_____

Question 9

The following is a sequence of tiling patterns.

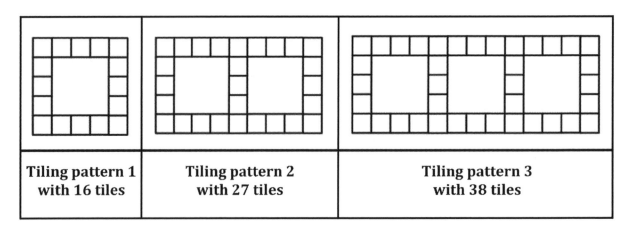

| Tiling pattern 1 with 16 tiles | Tiling pattern 2 with 27 tiles | Tiling pattern 3 with 38 tiles |

(a) Write down the number of tiles in patterns 4, 5 and 6.

Pattern 4:_____   Pattern 5:_____   Pattern 6:_____

(b) What do you notice about the number of tiles as the pattern number increases?

_____

_____

_____

_____

_____

_____

(c) Complete the sequence in the table below.

Pattern Number, N	Number of Tiles, T
1	5 + 11 = 16
2	5 + 22 = 27
3	5 + 33 = 38
4	
5	
6	
7	
8	

(d) Use your observations above to think of a formula for the number of tiles (T) in pattern number N. Write down your formula.

*Answer:*_____

(e) Which pattern number has 137 tiles?

*Answer:*_____

(f) How many tiles are there in pattern 10?

*Answer:*_____

Question 10

Each participant in the London Marathon wears a number. The numbers start from 1 and increase up to the total number of participants. No number is missed out and all the numbers are positive, whole numbers. If we count the number of digits in each participant's number and add these together, the total number of digits is 834. How many participants are there in total?

*Answer:*_____

Question 11

A group of children are standing in a circle. Each child has a number and they stand so that child 2 is next to child 1, child 3 is next to child 2, *and so on*. The children are evenly spaced and each child stands in a straight line directly opposite another child. A 67.5° angle is created at the intersection of the lines of child 4 and child 7.

(a) How many children are there in the circle?

*Answer:*_____

(b) Which child is opposite child 6?

*Answer:*_____

Some of the children decide to leave the circle. The remaining children receive new numbers and, as before, child 2 stands next to child 1, child 3 stands next to child 2, *etc*. This time we have a 90° angle between child 4 and child 7.

(c) How many children left the circle?

*Answer:*_____

(d) Which child is now opposite child 6?

*Answer:*_____

Question 12

(a) List all the **positive, whole numbers below 100** that have a remainder of 3 when divided by 4 and a remainder of 4 when divided by 5.

*Answer:*_____

(b) List all the **positive, whole numbers below 100** that have a remainder of 4 when divided by 5 and a remainder of 5 when divided by 6.

*Answer:*_____

(c) List all the **positive, whole numbers below 100** that have a remainder of 3 when divided by 4, a remainder of 4 when divided by 5 and a remainder of 5 when divided by 6.

*Answer:*_____

(d) List all the **positive, whole numbers below 400** that have a remainder of 3 when divided by 4, a remainder of 4 when divided by 5 and a remainder of 5 when divided by 6.

*Answer:*_____

(e) Look at your answers from part (d). What is the remainder when we divide the largest of these numbers by 7?

*Answer:*_____

Question 13

Three **identical, overlapping, equilateral triangles** are shown below with some of the lengths provided:

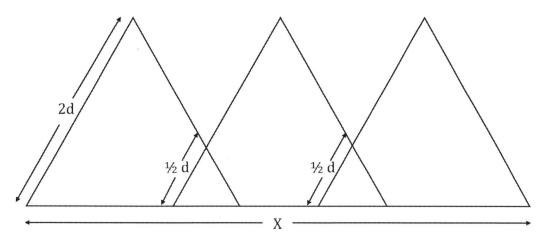

(a) Write down an expression for X in terms of d.

*Answer:*_____

(b) Write down an expression for the perimeter of the entire shape.

*Answer:*_____

If you examine our three overlapping triangles you will see that there are two smaller triangles that have been formed by the overlapping parts of the three large triangles. You are told that **the height of each of the large triangles = h** and **the height of each of the small triangles = 1/4 h.**

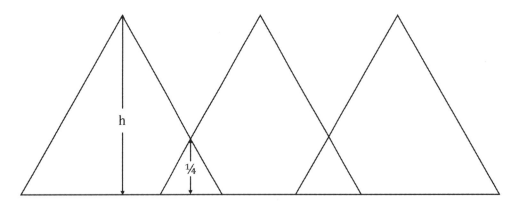

You are also told that **the area of any triangle = 1/2 × the base of the triangle × the height of the triangle**.

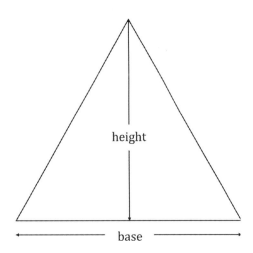

(c) Write down an expression for the area of the entire shape.

*Answer:*_____

Question 14

John, Jonah and Angus take 27 hours to build a brick wall. Jonah and Angus (without John), working just as hard as each other, together take 36 hours to build the same wall. How long would John take to build the wall on his own?

Answer:_____

Question 15

Tara enjoys drawing shapes. She draws the square and circle below and shades some sections in. The point A is at the center of both circle and square.

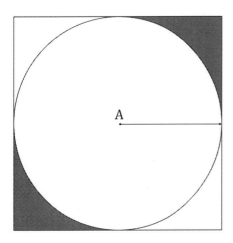

(a) If the area of the square is 400 cm², what is the radius of the circle?

*Answer:*_____

You are told that the area of a circle is πr^2, where r is the radius of the circle and π = 'pi' = 22/7.

(b) If the area of the square is 196 cm², find the area of the shaded region.

*Answer:*_____

Question 16

The letters A, B, C and D each stand for a **positive, whole number**. You are told that

A + B + C = 145
A + B + D = 187
B + C + D = 154
C + A + D = 180

What number does each letter represent?

A = _____　　*B* = _____　　*C* = _____　　*D* = _____

Question 17

There are five towns and five trains. Each train travels from one town to another. Each town has exactly one train that departs from it and one train that arrives. The blue train arrived at town A. The red train arrived at town B. The green train left from town C. The yellow train left from town B but did not go to town C. The white train left from town D. The yellow train did not go to town D. Fill in the blanks below to show the journey made by each train.

The _____ train left town _____ and arrived at town A.

The _____ train left town _____ and arrived at town B.

The _____ train left town _____ and arrived at town C.

The _____ train left town _____ and arrived at town D.

The _____ train left town _____ and arrived at town E.

Question 18

There are no more than 70 children in Willow class. During break all the children from Willow class like to play in groups. For one game they form groups of 5 and one child is left out. For another game they form groups of 8 and 4 children are left out. In a third game they form groups of 6 and everyone gets a chance to play. How many children are there in Willow class?

*Answer:*_____

Question 19

(a) A, B and C each represent a single digit with no two digits being the same. Find the values of A, B and C so that the following are true:

A B + C = 38 _____ (1)

B C + A = 29 _____ (2)

A = _____   *B =* _____   *C =* _____

(b) A, B, C, D and E each represent a single digit with no two digits being the same. Find their values so that the following are true:

A B C D + E = 3860 _____ (1)

C E D B + A = 5651 _____ (2)

A = _____   *B =* _____   *C =* _____   *D =* _____   *E =* _____

Question 20

A number generator produces a sequence of numbers by following a special rule, however some of the numbers are missing.

(a) Fill in the missing numbers.

0,   3,   8,   15, _____,   35,   48, _____,   80

(b) What is the number generator's rule for this sequence?

*Answer:*_____

Question 21

Two lorries travelled 540 km from Town A to Town B along the same road. The first lorry left Town A at 6 a.m. and maintained an average speed of 60 km/hour. The second lorry left Town A 90 minutes later and arrived at Town B 90 minutes before the first lorry.

(a) Work out the average speed of the second lorry.

*Answer:*_____

(b) At what time did the second lorry pass the first lorry?

*Answer:*_____

(c) What was the distance between the two lorries at 12 noon?

*Answer:*_____

Question 22

Karim draws a picture of two circles and a square. The points O and P are at the center of the circles. The area of the square given by the points O, A, P and B is 196 cm².

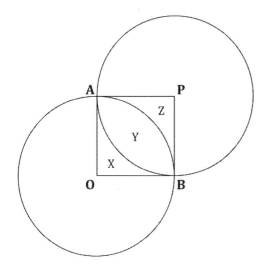

You are told that the area of a circle is given by πr^2, where π = 'pi' = 22/7.

(a) Find the overlapping area of the two circles, *i.e.* area Y.

*Answer:*_____

(b) Find the perimeter of area Y.

*Answer:*_____

Question 23

Jacob has five red cars and five black cars.

(a) In how many ways can he arrange a row of five cars so that no two adjacent cars are the same colour?

*Answer:*_____

(b) In how many ways can he arrange a row of five cars so that no two adjacent cars are red?

*Answer:*_____

Question 24

You are given a calculator for which only 7 buttons work.

| C | = | 3 | 6 | 8 | × | – |

You can use any button as many times as you like.

Starting with the clear button C, show how to use the remaining six buttons to arrive at the answers shown below:

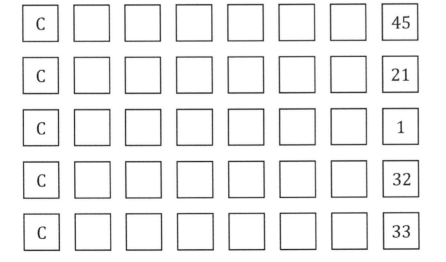

Question 25

Here is a sequence of patterns made from rectangles and triangles.

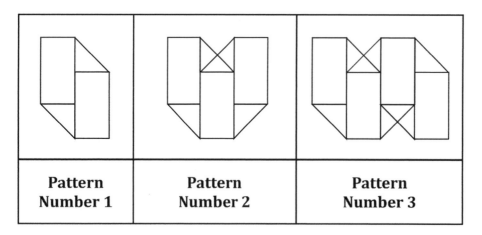

| Pattern Number 1 | Pattern Number 2 | Pattern Number 3 |

The sequence continues in the same way.

(a) Draw a picture of pattern number 5.

(b) What is the rule connecting the number of rectangles and the pattern number?

*The rule is:*_____

_____

_____

_____

(c) What is the rule connecting the number of triangles and the pattern number?

*The rule is:*_____

_____

_____

_____

(d) How many triangles are there in pattern 8?

*Answer:*_____

(e) One pattern has 12 rectangles. How many triangles are there in this pattern?

*Answer:*_____

(f) Which pattern has 47 triangles?

*Answer:*_____

Question 26

Yseult draws a circle of radius 6 cm and shades some sections in.

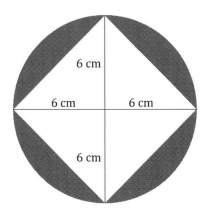

You are told that the area of a circle is given by πr^2, where π = 'pi' = 22/7. What is the total area of the shaded parts?

*Answer:*_____

Question 27

26 divided by 3 gives us 8 plus a remainder of 2. We can write this as 26 ÷ 3 = 8 R 2.

(a) Fill in the blank boxes in the tables below.

						R	
31	÷	7	=			R	
58	÷	7	=			R	
89	÷	7	=			R	

						R	
66	÷	4	=			R	
41	÷	4	=			R	
107	÷	4	=			R	

(b) Examine your answers in the tables above. You are told that 76,545,654,563 + 46,969,632,691 = 123,515,287,254. Use the information in the table below to work out 123,515,287,254 ÷ 379. **Do not perform the division or use a calculator**. Write your answer in the blank boxes.

					R	
76,545,654,563	÷	379	=	201,967,426	R	109
46,969,632,691	÷	379	=	123,930,429	R	100
123,515,287,254	÷	379	=		R	

(c) You are now told that 76,545,654,563 − 46,969,632,691 = 29,576,021,872. Use the information in the table below to work out 29,576,021,872 ÷ 379. **Do not perform the division or use a calculator.** Write your answer in the blank boxes.

76,545,654,563	÷	379	=	201,967,426	R	109
46,969,632,691	÷	379	=	123,930,429	R	100
29,576,021,872	÷	379	=		R	

(d) Fill in the blanks below. Use the information provided above to help you. **Do not perform the division or use a calculator.**

76,545,654,863	÷	379	=		R	

(e) Fill in the blanks below. Use the information provided above to help you. **Do not perform the division or use a calculator.**

46,969,632,291	÷	379	=		R	

Question 28

(a) Find ten **consecutive integers** that add up to 5. The integers may include negative numbers, positive numbers and zeros.

*Answer:*_____

_____

_____

(b) What is the 10th term in a sequence of 16 **consecutive integers** (positive, negative or zero) that add up to 8? Which term is the largest term and what is the value of that term?

*Answer:*_____

_____

_____

(c) Identify the rule that governs the following sequence and find the next 2 terms:

−2,   1,   −2,   4,   −8,   64, ____, ____

The rule is: _____

_____

_____

_____

Question 29

A leaky tank is 75% full. 25% of the remaining water leaks out leaving 3,393 litres of water. The capacity of the tank is the volume of water that the tank holds when it is completely full.

(a) What is the capacity of the tank?

*Answer:*_____

At the start of each week a different tank is filled to capacity with water. By the end of the week 1/3 of the original volume of water has been lost due to a leak and there remains 63 litres of water.

(b) What is the capacity of the tank?

*Answer:*_____

Question 30

Jake receives two clocks for Christmas. The red clock is currently 25 minutes ahead of the correct time and loses 7½ seconds every hour. The blue clock is currently 14½ minutes behind the correct time and gains 15 seconds every ½ hour.

(a) How long will it take for the red clock to show the correct time?

*Answer:*_____

(b) How long will it take for the blue clock to show the correct time?

*Answer:*_____

(c) Jake sets the red clock to show the correct time at 22:30 on Friday. What time will the red clock show when it is 14:30 on Saturday?

*Answer:*_____

(d) Jake sets the blue clock to show the correct time at 10:50 on Friday. What is the correct time when the blue clock is showing 20:55 on the same day?

*Answer:*_____

(e) The football match is shown on TV at 19:30 every Saturday. On the day before the match (Friday) Jake re-sets the red clock to show the correct time at 19:30. How much of the match will he miss if he does not re-set the red clock again and he goes by the time showing on this clock?

*Answer:*_____

Answers

Answer 1

(a) Jason will need 12 black cubes to go around the outside of his white sculpture.

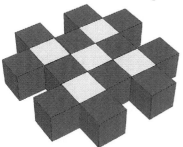

He will need another 5 black cubes to go over the top of his white sculpture.

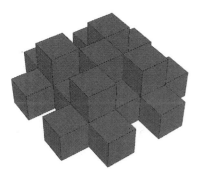

Finally he will need 5 more black cubes to cover the exposed white faces on the underside of his sculpture.

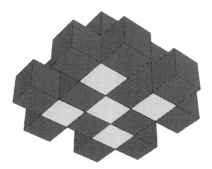

So Jason will need a total of **22 black cubes** to cover all the exposed faces of his white sculpture.

(b) Following a similar way of thinking it is possible to show that Jason will now need a total of **50 red cubes** to cover all the exposed faces of his black sculpture.

Answer 2

(a) Let $a\,b\,c\,d\,e\,f\,g\,h$ represent the 8-digit code. We are told that each group of six adjacent digits adds to 24 and each group of five adjacent digits adds to 20. Let's consider the first five adjacent digits, which are $a\,b\,c\,d\,e$. These five digits sum to 20. The first six adjacent digits are $a\,b\,c\,d\,e\,f$ and these six digits sum to 24. Therefore f must be 4. Now let's consider the second five adjacent digits $b\,c\,d\,e\,f$. These sum to 20. Since each group of six adjacent digits sums to 24 then a must be 4 and g must also be 4. Continuing like this: the five adjacent digits $c\,d\,e\,f\,g$ add to 20 therefore $b = h = 4$; and the five adjacent digits $d\,e\,f\,g\,h$ add to 20 therefore $c = 4$. We have established so far that the 8-digit code has to be 4 4 4 $d\,e$ 4 4 4. Furthermore it must be the case that d and e sum to 8 since each group of five adjacent digits adds to 20. The sum of all eight digits must therefore be 32.

(b) The 4th and 5th digits always sum to 8 and there are 7 possible combinations of **positive integers** that sum to 8. They are (1, 7), (2, 6), (3, 5), (4, 4), (5, 3), (6, 2), and (7, 1).

(c) We are told that the list starts with a d followed by an e, that the two d's are separated by 3 letters and that the two e's are separated by 4 letters. We can therefore start with the following: d, e, __, __, d, __ e, __, __, __. We are also told that the two a's are next to each other, the two b's are separated by one letter and the two c's are separated by two letters. The only sequence that satisfies all these conditions is **d, e, a, a, d, c e, b, c, b**.

Answer 3

(a) Since the lighthouses flash every 4, 5, 6 and 7 seconds respectively, we need to find the **lowest common multiple** of the numbers 4, 5, 6 and 7, *i.e.* the **smallest number** that is a **multiple of each of the numbers 4, 5, 6 and 7**.

The multiples of 4 are 4, 8, 12, 16, 20, 24, 28, ... *etc*
The multiples of 5 are 5, 10, 15, 20, 25, 30, 35, 40, ... *etc*
The multiples of 6 are 6, 12, 18, 24, 30, 36, 42, ... *etc*
The multiples of 7 are 7, 14, 21, 28, 35, 42, ... *etc*

The lowest common multiple of 4 and 5 is 20. The lowest common multiple of 4, 5 and 6 is 60. The lowest common multiple of 4, 5, 6 and 7 is 420. Therefore the next time all the lighthouses flash together will be 420 seconds (or 7 minutes) after the first time they flashed together. Since they first flashed together at exactly midnight (or 00:00), the next time they will flash together will be at 7 minutes past midnight (or 00:07).

(b) This time we need to find the **lowest common multiple** of the numbers 1, 2, 3, 4, 5 and 6. The lowest common multiple of these numbers is 60 so this means that the next time they all play together will be on **the 60th day after the 21st of March**. Since March has 31 days and April has 30 days, the next time they all play together will be on the 20th May.

Answer 4

Note - when we write a number next to a symbol this tells us how many of that particular symbol we have, so 2◉ tells us we have '2 of ◉' which is the same as ◉ + ◉.

The following information can be established from the table.

$$2◉ + ♥ = 100 \qquad\qquad \text{_____(1)}$$

$$2◉ + 2✓ = 132 \qquad\qquad \text{_____(2)}$$

$$2✓ + ♥ = 124 \qquad\qquad \text{_____(3)}$$

We can use this information to find the values of ◉, ♥ and ✓.

Adding equations (1) and (2) together gives us 4◉ + ♥ + 2✓ = 232. Let's call this equation (4).

Equation (3) tells us that 2✓ + ♥ = 124 so we can replace 2✓ + ♥ in equation (4) with 124. This gives us 4◉ + 124 = 232 or ◉ = 27.

Since ◉ = 27 we can replace ◉ in equations (1) and (2) to find ♥ = 100 − 54 = 46 and ✓ = 78 ÷ 2 = 39.

Now that we have found ◉ = 27, ♥ = 46 and ✓ = 39 we can now find **X** and **Y** as follows:

X = ◉ + 2✓ + ♥ = 27 + (2 × 39) + 46 = 27 + 78 + 46 = 151
and
Y = ◉ + 2♥ = 27 + (2 × 46) = 119.

<u>Summary of results</u>

◉ = 27   ♥ = 46   ✓ = 39   **X** = 151   **Y** = 119

Answer 5

(a) Let point X represent the point at which the two planes meet. We are told that plane B flies at an average speed of 240 km/hour. So plane B flies 40 km in the first 10 minutes after reaching point X and then flies another 20 km to reach Island A, making it a total of 60 km between point X and Island A. This means that plane A flew 60 km in the first 30 minutes and then flew 10 more minutes to get to Island B. If plane A flew 60 km in 30 minutes it would therefore fly 20 km in the remaining 10 minutes, so the total distance between the two islands must be 60 km + 20 km = 80 km.

(b) If plane A set out from Island A at 14:20 and took 40 minutes to get to Island B then it must have landed at 15:00. At this time plane B was 20 km away from landing at Island A and has therefore covered a distance of 80 km – 20 km = 60 km. Given a speed of 240 km/hour this means that plane B has been travelling for 15 minutes. This gives a departure time for plane B of 14:45.

Answer 6

(a) The remainders from the first two rows in the table tell us how many widgets were still without crates after the first and second batch of crates were ordered. If we add the remainders from the first two rows we see that a total of 960 widgets were still without crates.

(b) 2 more crates are required.

(c) A total of 20,241,383 crates are required for all the widgets.

(d) Once we take account of the damaged widgets only (20,241,382 – 4,974,874) + 1 crates will be required.

(e) The last crate contains 390 – 141 = 249 widgets.

(f) There are **400 more** damaged widgets than initially thought. Since the last crate previously had 249 widgets only 1 less crate is now needed. The number of crates that will be needed is therefore 20,241,382 – 4,974,874 which is 1 less than in (d).

(g) In (e), the final crate had 249 widgets, however there are now **400 fewer** widgets needing to be shipped therefore this final crate will no longer be needed. The new, final crate will have only 570 – (400 – 249) = 419 widgets.

Answer 7

(a) Circle A is the smallest circle and has a radius of 9 cm. Since the radii of the circles are in the ratios of 1:2:3:4:5:6, this means that the radius of circle B is twice the radius of circle A, the radius of circle C is 3 times the radius of circle A, *and so on*. The radius of circle D is therefore 4 times the radius of circle A, and so the radius of circle D must be 4 × 9 cm = 36 cm.

(b) The area of the largest shaded part is given by the area of circle F *minus* the area of circle E. The area of each circle is πr^2, where r is the radius and π = 'pi' = 22/7. The radius of circle F is 6 × 9 cm = 54 cm and the radius of circle E is 5 × 9 cm = 45 cm. Therefore the area of the largest shaded part must be

Area of circle F – area of circle E
= (π × 54 cm × 54 cm) – (π × 45 cm × 45 cm)
= 22/7 × [(54 cm × 54 cm) – (45 cm × 45 cm)]
= 22/7 × [2,916 cm^2 – 2,025 cm^2]
= 22/7 × 891 cm^2
= 2,800.3 cm^2

(c) The total perimeter of all the circles is

2 × 22/7 × [9 cm + 18 cm + 27 cm + 36 cm + 45 cm + 54 cm]
= 2 × 22/7 × 189 cm
= 1,188 cm.

Answer 8

A sensible way to approach this question is to start by looking for symbols that might represent either a 0 or 1. Any symbol times one produces itself. Any symbol times zero produces zero. You can also look for symbols that are multiplied by themselves. These produce square numbers such as 1, 4, 9, 16, *etc*. By taking this approach you can check to see that the following are true:

♥ = 0   △ = 5

◇ = 1   ⊕ = 6

▲ = 2   Φ = 7

▮ = 3   ⊙ = 8

✚ = 4   ⊞ = 9

Answer 9

(a)
Pattern 4: 49 tiles
Pattern 5: 60 tiles
Pattern 6: 71 tiles

(b) Each pattern adds 11 tiles to the preceding pattern. We can think of pattern 1 as made up of 5 tiles arranged vertically along the left hand side with another 11 tiles added on. Pattern 2 then adds another 11 tiles to pattern 1, so we can think of pattern 2 as made up of 5 tiles with 11 + 11 = 2 × 11 = 22 tiles added on, *and so on*.

(c)

Pattern Number, N	Number of Tiles, T
1	5 + 11 = 16
2	5 + 22 = 27
3	5 + 33 = 38
4	5 + 44 = 49
5	5 + 55 = 60
6	5 + 66 = 71
7	5 + 77 = 82
8	5 + 88 = 93

(d) Pattern number N is made up of 5 tiles plus another N × 11 tiles added on, so our formula must be T = 5 + (11 × N).

(e) You can use the formula to work this out. If there are 137 tiles then T = 137 and so N must equal 12, therefore **pattern number 12** has 137 tiles.

(f) If the pattern number is 10 then using our formula we have N = 10 and so T must be 115. Therefore pattern number 10 has **115 tiles**.

Answer 10

There are 314 participants altogether.

Participants with 1 digit	9 participants: Numbers 1 to 9	Number of digits = 9
Participants with 2 digits	90 participants: Numbers 10 to 99	Number of digits = 90 × 2 = 180
Participants with 3 digits	215 participants: Numbers 100 to 314	Number of digits = 215 × 3 = 645
	Total number of participants = 314	**Total number of digits = 834**

Answer 11

(a) First draw a picture to represent the information provided *(not drawn to scale)*.

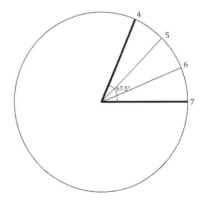

The 67.5° angle represents the angle at the intersection of the lines of child 4 and child 7. Child 5 and child 6 lie between child 4 and child 7 and all the children are evenly spaced, so child 5 and child 6 dissect the 67.5° angle into 3 equal

angles. Each of these angles must be 22.5° and so the angle at the intersection of the lines of **any 2 neighbouring children** must also be 22.5°. There must therefore be 16 children in total since 22.5° × 16 = 360° *(see picture below)*.

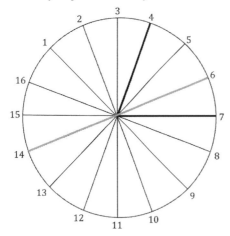

(b) From the picture above we see that child 14 is opposite child 6.

(c) Draw a new picture showing the new lines of child 4 and child 7. These lines intersect at 90° and there are 2 children (child 5 and child 6) between child 4 and child 7 *(not drawn to scale)*.

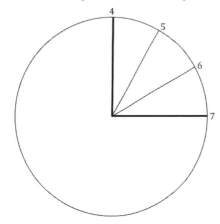

Since the children are evenly spaced, the angle at the intersection of the lines of **any 2 neighbouring children** must now be 30°. We can continue drawing lines and children until we see that there must now be only 12 children remaining in the circle *(see picture below)*. Since there were 16 children before, then 4 children must have left the circle.

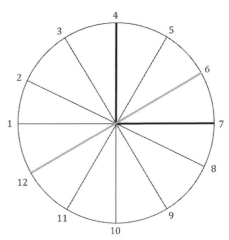

(d) This time child 12 is opposite child 6.

Answer 12

(a) The numbers we are looking for are the set of numbers, up to 100, that are **1 less than the *common multiples of 4 and 5***. This will ensure that we get a remainder of 3 when divided by 4 **and** a remainder of 4 when divided by 5. The numbers up to 100 that are multiples of both 4 and 5 (*i.e.* the common multiples of 4 and 5) are 20, 40, 60, 80 and 100. Therefore the numbers we are looking for must be <u>19, 39, 59, 79 and 99</u>. You can check to see that these numbers produce a remainder of 3 when divided by 4 **and** a remainder of 4 when divided by 5.

(b) This time the numbers we are looking for must satisfy the conditions of being **1 less than the *common multiples of 5 and 6*** as well as being no greater than 100. The numbers up to 100 that are multiples of both 5 and 6 are 30, 60 and 90, so the numbers we are looking for must be <u>29, 59 and 89</u>. Check to see that these numbers produce a remainder of 4 when divided by 5 **and** a remainder of 5 when divided by 6.

(c) The number(s) we are looking for must be those numbers that satisfied **both** (a) and (b) above. This number is <u>59</u>.

(d) This time we need to consider **all the common multiples up to 400 of 4, 5 and 6**. The numbers we are looking for are the numbers that are 1 less than each of these common multiples. This will ensure that we get a remainder of 3 when divided by 4, a remainder of 4 when divided by 5 **and** a remainder of 5 when divided by 6. The common multiples up to 400 of 4, 5 and 6 are 60, 120, 180, 240, 300 and 360 therefore the numbers we are looking for are <u>59, 119, 179, 239, 299 and 359</u>.

(e) The largest of the numbers from (d) is 359. The remainder when we divide 359 by 7 is <u>2</u>.

Answer 13

(a) Since each of the three overlapping triangles is **identical and equilateral**, all their sides measure 2d and all their angles are the same at 60°. In the picture below line WV is parallel to line YZ and so the angles at W and V are the same as the angles at Y and Z. This means that all the angles throughout the picture must be the same at 60°.

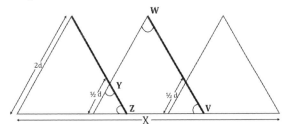

Therefore the two small triangles formed by the overlapping areas must both be equilateral and each of their three sides must measure ½d. The length of X is therefore given by 3 lots of 2d *takeaway* 2 lots of ½d = 6d − d = 5d.

(b) The perimeter of the entire shape is 15d.

(c) The area of each of the large triangles is ½ × base × height = ½ × 2d × h = dh. The area of each of the small triangles is ½ × base × height = ½ × ½d × ¼h = 1/16 × dh. The total area of the entire shape is therefore

3 lots of dh *takeaway* 2 lots of (1/16 × dh)

= (3 × dh) − (2 × 1/16 × dh)

= (3 × dh) − (1/8 × dh)

= (2 + 7/8) × dh.

Answer 14

Jonah and Angus (without John) together took 36 hours to build the entire wall, so in one hour they would have completed 1/36 of the wall. This means that in 27 hours Jonah and Angus would have completed 27/36 = ¾ of the wall. However when Jonah and Angus work with John, the entire wall is built in 27 hours so John must have completed the remaining ¼ of the wall in 27 hours. This means John would need 27 hours × 4 = 108 hours to build the whole wall on his own.

Answer 15

(a) If the area of the square is 400 cm², then each side of the square must be 20 cm (since 20 cm × 20 cm = 400 cm²) and the radius of the circle must be ½ × 20 cm = 10 cm.

(b) If the area of the square is 196 cm², then each side of the square must be 14 cm and the radius of the circle must be ½ × 14 cm = 7 cm. The area of the circle must therefore be πr^2 = 22/7 × 7 cm × 7 cm = 154 cm². The shaded area must therefore be

½ × (the area of the square − the area of the circle)

= ½ × (196 cm² − 154 cm²)

= ½ × 42 cm²

= 21 cm².

Answer 16

We can add these 4 equations together to get 3 × (A + B + C + D) = 666 or A + B + C + D = 222. We can use this last result plus the information we were given to work out the values of A, B, C and D:

A = 222 − 154 = 68
B = 222 − 180 = 42
C = 222 − 187 = 35
D = 222 − 145 = 77

Answer 17

First let's start by creating a table to organize all the information we've been given. Our table may look something like this:

Departures		Arrivals	
Town A	?	Town A	Blue
Town B	Yellow	Town B	Red
Town C	Green	Town C	?
Town D	White	Town D	?
Town E	?	Town E	?

We were also told that the yellow train did not arrive at either of towns C or D. Since it also did not arrive at towns A or B then it must have arrived at town E. Since the green train left town C it must have arrived at town D (since all trains leave from one town and arrive at another). Likewise the white train must have arrived at town C. The blue train could not have left from town A since it arrived at town A, therefore it must have left from town E. Finally the red train must have left from town A. We can therefore fill in the missing information in our table as follows:

Departures		Arrivals	
Town A	Red	Town A	Blue
Town B	Yellow	Town B	Red
Town C	Green	Town C	White
Town D	White	Town D	Green
Town E	Blue	Town E	Yellow

Alternatively we can write:

The BLUE train left town E and arrived at town A
The RED train left town A and arrived at town B
The WHITE train left town D and arrived at town C
The GREEN train left town C and arrived at town D
The YELLOW train left town B and arrived at town E

Answer 18

The answer must be a number no greater than 70. It must also be a multiple of 6 because when the children formed groups of 6 no one was left out. The number must also be such that when divided by 5 leaves a remainder of 1 and when divided by 8 leaves a remainder of 4. We can check all the multiples of 6 that are no greater than 70 to see which number also satisfies all the remaining conditions. The only number to satisfy all the conditions is 36, so there must be 36 children in Willow class.

Answer 19

(a) Let us re-write the information provided in the two equations in the following way:

Equation 1	**Equation 2**

$$\begin{array}{cc} A & B \\ + & C \\ \hline 3 & 8 \end{array} \qquad \begin{array}{cc} B & C \\ + & A \\ \hline 2 & 9 \end{array}$$

From equation 1 we see that the digit A can't be bigger than 3, so it has to be 3, 2 or 1. <u>Suppose A = 1</u>, then from equation 2 we must have C = 8 and B = 2, but according to the first equation this can't be correct therefore A can't be 1. <u>Suppose A = 2</u>, then from the second equation we must have C = 7 and B = 2 however according to the first equation this can't be correct therefore A can't be 2. <u>This leaves us with A = 3</u>: if A = 3 then C = 6 and B = 2 and with these values both equations are now simultaneously correct:

A B + C = 32 + 6 = 38   _____ (1)

B C + A = 26 + 3 = 29   _____ (2)

(b) From the first equation we see that the digits D and E must add to 10. This means the <u>digit C must be 5</u> and the <u>digits A and B must be 3 and 8</u> <u>respectively</u>. From the second equation, if A and B are 3 and 8 respectively then they must add to 11 and so the <u>digit D must be 4</u> and the <u>digit E must be 6</u>. We can check to see that with these values both equations are simultaneously correct:

ABCD + E = 3854 + 6 = 3860   _____ (1)

CEDB + A = 5648 + 3 = 5651   _____ (2)

Answer 20

(a) The missing numbers are 24 and 63. The complete sequence is:

0, 3, 8, 15, **24**, 35, 48, **63**, 80

(b) The rule for the number in position n is $n^2 - 1$.

Answer 21

(a) The first lorry, travelling at 60 km/hour, would take 9 hours to get to Town B so it must have got there at 3 pm. The second lorry left 90 minutes later and arrived 90 minutes earlier, so it must have left Town A at 7.30 a.m. and arrived at Town B at 1.30 p.m. This means it took 6 hours to travel the distance of 540 km between Town A and Town B, so it must have been travelling at 90 km/hour.

(b) When the second lorry left at 7.30 a.m. the first lorry had already been travelling for 1 and ½ hours. At 60 km/hour this means that the first lorry had already travelled a distance of 90 km. By 8.30 a.m. the first lorry would now have travelled a distance of 90 km (since it travels 90 km/hour)

while the second lorry would have travelled a total distance of 90 km + 60 km = 150 km. We can continue examining the distances travelled by both lorries at periodic intervals and put our results in a table as follows:

	7.30 am	8.30 am	9.30 am	10.30 am	11.30 am	...
Distance covered by 1st lorry	90 km	150 km	210 km	270 km	330 km	etc.
Distance covered by 2nd lorry	0 km	90 km	180 km	270 km	360 km	etc.

If we examine our results we notice that at 10.30 a.m. the second lorry has just caught up with the first lorry because they have both covered the same distance of 270 km. Therefore the second lorry passes the first lorry at 10.30 a.m.

(c) We can extend our table above to work out the distances travelled by both lorries at 12 noon. At 12 noon the first lorry has travelled 360 km and the second lorry has travelled 405 km, therefore the second lorry was 45 kilometers ahead of the first lorry.

Answer 22

(a) The area of the square is 196 cm² therefore each side of the square must be 14 cm (since 14 cm × 14 cm = 196 cm²) and this must also be the radius, r, of the two circles. The area of a circle is given by πr^2, where π = 'pi' = 22/7, so the area of each of the circles is 22/7 × 14 cm × 14 cm = 616 cm². The area of the quadrant OAB (= area X + area Y) is one quarter of the area of the entire circle, so the area of the quadrant OAB is ¼ × 616 cm² = 154 cm². This is the same as the area of the quadrant PAB (= area Y + area Z). The area Y is therefore

[(Area X + area Y) + (area Y + area Z)] − (area X + area Y + area Z)

= (Area of quadrant OAB + area of quadrant PAB) − area of the square

= (154 cm² + 154 cm²) − 196 cm²

= 308 cm² − 196 cm²

= 112 cm².

(b) The perimeter of the circle is $2\pi r = 2 \times 22/7 \times 14$ cm = 88 cm. The perimeter of the arc AB must be ¼ of the perimeter of the circle = ¼ × 88 cm = 22 cm. The perimeter of the area Y must be 2 × the perimeter of the arc AB = 2 × 22 cm = 44 cm.

Answer 23

(a) In Jacob's row of 5 cars there can't be more than 3 cars of the same colour. If not – suppose there were 4 or 5 cars of any given colour, then it wouldn't be possible to prevent two cars of the same colour being adjacent. The only possibilities therefore for Jacob's row of cars are either '2 red and 3 black' cars or '2 black and 3 red' cars. In either case there is only one possible arrangement such that no two adjacent cars are the same colour. This is the arrangement whereby cars alternate in colour - 'red, black, red, black, red' or 'black, red, black, red, black' - so there is a total of 2 possibilities altogether.

(b) This time Jacob's row of 5 cars must always have at least two black cars. If not - suppose there were no black cars, then we would end up with five red cars and it wouldn't be possible to prevent two of them from being adjacent; suppose there was just one black car, then we would end up with four red cars and again it wouldn't be possible to prevent two of them from being adjacent. The possibilities this time are therefore either '2 black and 3 red', '3 black and 2 red', '4 black and 1 red' or '5 black and no red' cars. These possibilities are set out in the table below and this time we see that there are a total of 13 possible arrangements so that no two adjacent cars are red:

Number of black cars	Number of red cars	Number of possible arrangements
2	3	1
3	2	6
4	1	5
5	0	1
Total number of possible arrangements		**13**

Answer 24

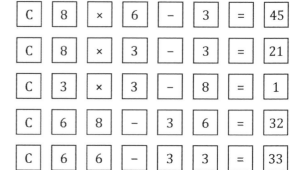

Answer 25

(a) Pattern number 5 looks like this:

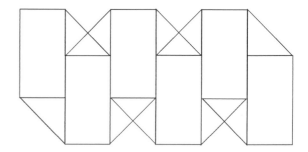

(b) If we examine the sequence of patterns we see that pattern 1 has 2 rectangles, pattern 2 has 3 rectangles, pattern 3 has 4 rectangles, *and so on*, therefore the number of rectangles (R) in any pattern is always 1 + the pattern number (N), *i.e.* R = N + 1.

(c) First notice that whenever two of the larger triangles overlap they create three smaller triangles. We can count the number of triangles in each pattern and put our results in a table such as the one below:

Pattern Number	1	2	3	4
Number of LARGER triangles	2	4	6	8
Number of SMALLER triangles	0	3	6	9
TOTAL number of triangles	2	7	12	17

This table shows the number of larger triangles, the number of smaller triangles and the total number of triangles in each pattern. If we do this for the first few patterns we begin to notice that the number of larger triangles in any pattern is always 2 × the pattern number and the number of smaller triangles in any pattern is always 3 × (the pattern number − 1). The total number of triangles (T) in any pattern (N) is therefore T = 2N + 3(N − 1) = 5N − 3.

(d) Since T = 5N − 3 then in pattern 8 (*i.e.* N = 8) there must be a total of 37 triangles (including both large and small triangles).

(e) The pattern with 12 rectangles must be pattern 11. In pattern 11 (*i.e.* N = 11) the total number of triangles is T = 5N − 3 = (5 × 11) − 3 = 52 triangles.

(f) If there are 47 triangles then T = 5N − 3 = 47 and therefore N = 10. <u>Alternatively</u>: From the table in part (c) we see that the total number of triangles increases by 5 in each subsequent pattern, therefore if pattern 11 has 52 triangles (we found this out in part (e)), then the pattern with 47 triangles must be the pattern just before, *i.e.* pattern 10.

Answer 26

Let r represent the radius of the circle and π represent 'pi' = 22/7. The area of a circle is given by πr^2, so the area of Yseult's circle must be 22/7 × 6 cm × 6 cm = 113.1 cm². The area of a triangle is given by ½ × **the base of the triangle × the height of the triangle**, so the area of each of the triangles is ½ × 6 cm × 6 cm = 18 cm². Since the square is made up of 4 triangles then the area of the square must be 4 × 18 cm² = 72 cm². The area of the shaded parts must therefore be the area of

the circle minus the area of the square = 113.1 cm² − 72 cm² = 41.1 cm².

Answer 27

(a)

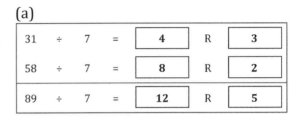

31	÷	7	=	4	R	3
58	÷	7	=	8	R	2
89	÷	7	=	12	R	5

66	÷	4	=	16	R	2
41	÷	4	=	10	R	1
107	÷	4	=	26	R	3

(b) The new numerator is the sum of the two original numerators in the information we were given, therefore the answer is the sum of the two original results and the new remainder is the sum of the two original remainders.

76,545,654,563	÷	379	=	201,967,426	R	109
46,969,632,691	÷	379	=	123,930,429	R	100
123,515,287,254	÷	379	=	**325,897,855**	R	**209**

(c) This time the new numerator is the difference between the two original numerators in the information we were given, so the answer is the difference between the two original results and the remainder is the difference between the two original remainders.

76,545,654,563	÷	379	=	201,967,426	R	109
46,969,632,691	÷	379	=	123,930,429	R	100
29,576,021,872	÷	379	=	**78,036,997**	R	**9**

(d) Here the numerator is 300 more than the numerator in the first equation, so the remainder increases by 300. However this means that the remainder becomes 409, which is greater than the denominator of 379 therefore we increase our result by 1 and our remainder just becomes 30.

| 76,545,654,863 | ÷ | 379 | = | **201,967,427** | R | **30** |

(e) This time our numerator is 400 less than the numerator in the second equation. Let's see what happens if we make sequential changes to the value of this numerator. Suppose, instead, we had reduced the numerator by only 100. Then our result would have been the same as the original result but with no remainder. If we then reduced the numerator by a further 379 (so we have now reduced it by a total of 479) our new result would become 1 less than the original result, again with no remainder. If we now finally increase the numerator by 79 (so we have finally reduced it by a total of 400 exactly) we would get no change to our previous result however we would have a remainder of 79.

| 46,969,632,291 | ÷ | 379 | = | **123,930,428** | R | **79** |

Answer 28

(a) The ten **consecutive integers** (positive, negative or zero) that add up to 5 are −4, −3, −2, −1, 0, 1, 2, 3, 4, and 5.

(b) The 16 **consecutive integers** (positive, negative or zero) that add up to 8 are −7, −6, −5, −4, −3, −2, −1, 0, 1, **2**, 3, 4, 5, 6, 7 and **8**. The 10th term in the sequence is 2. The largest term is the last or 16th term and its value is 8.

(c) The rule that governs the sequence is: 'after the first 3 terms, the next term is the product of the preceding 3 terms'. The complete sequence, including the next two terms, is −2, 1, −2, 4, −8, 64, **−2,048** and **1,048,576**.

Answer 29

(a) Let X represent the full capacity of the tank. If the information we've been given is correct then it

must be the case that $(X − ¼X) − ¼(X − ¼X) = ¾X − ¼(¾X) = ¾ × ¾ × X = 3,393$ litres or $X = 3,393$ litres $× 4/3 × 4/3 = 3,393$ litres $× 16/9 = 377$ litres $× 16 = 6,032$ litres. Therefore the full capacity of the tank is 6,032 litres.

(b) Let X represent the full capacity of the tank. Since 63 litres represent 2/3 of the full capacity of the tank, then $2/3 × X = 63$ litres and therefore $X = (63 × 3) ÷ 2 = 189 ÷ 2 = 94.5$ litres.

Answer 30

(a) The red clock must lose 25 minutes (= 1,500 seconds) in order to show the correct time. It loses 7½ seconds every hour so it will take 200 hours (or 8 days and 8 hours) to lose 1,500 seconds and show the correct time.

(b) The blue clock is currently 14½ minutes (= 870 seconds) behind the correct time so it needs to gain 870 seconds in order to show the correct time. It gains 15 seconds every ½ hour (or 30 seconds every hour), therefore it will take 29 hours for the blue clock to show the correct time.

(c) The red clock loses 7½ seconds every hour, so it takes 8 hours to lose 1 minute or 16 hours to lose 2 minutes. 16 hours have elapsed between 22:30 on Friday and 14:30 on Saturday, so the red clock will have lost two minutes during these 16 hours. It will therefore be showing 14:28 when the correct time on Saturday is 14.30.

(d) The blue clock gains 15 seconds every ½ hour. This is the same as gaining 1 minute every 2 hours. At 10:50 the clock was set to show 10:50. At 12:50 the clock would therefore be showing 12:51. At 14:50 the clock would be showing 14:52, *and so on.* At 18:50 the clock would be showing 18:54 and at 20:50 the clock would be showing 20:55. So when the blue clock is showing 20:55, the actual time is 20:50.

(e) The red clock loses 7½ seconds every hour. This is equivalent to losing 3 minutes every 24 hours, so by 19:30 on Saturday the red clock will be showing 19:27. Jake will therefore miss the first 3 minutes of the match if he goes by the time on the red clock.